Contents

Any words appearing in bold, **like this**, are explained in the Glossary

Introduction

What kinds of music are brass instruments used for?

You will find brass instruments in many different kinds of music. In big classical orchestras, the brass section will usually contain trumpets, trombones and French horns. There may also be a tuba, and possibly some other less well-known instruments, depending on the piece of music the orchestra is playing. In small jazz groups, there may be a trumpet or a trombone or both; traditional jazz groups may include a tuba or sousaphone, which will play the **bass part**. A typical jazz orchestra or '**big band**' will usually include a trumpet section (one or more of the players may also play flugelhorn) and a trombone section (one will be a bass trombone).

Contemporary jazz bands of all sizes can also include a French horn, a tuba or any other brass instrument – for example, the **tenor** horn, which is more often used in brass bands and marching bands. Horn sections used in rock, pop and Latin music will usually include a trumpet and possibly a trombone, as well as one or more saxophone. Although saxophones are made of brass, they are classed as **woodwind** instruments, because their sound is made by a **reed**, in the same way as the clarinet.

The brass section of an orchestra. Can you name the instruments?

SOUNDBITES

Brass

Roger Thomas

Heinemann
LIBRARY

www.heinemann.co.uk/library
Visit our website to find out more information about Heinemann Library books.

To order:
☎ Phone 44 (0) 1865 888066
🖹 Send a fax to 44 (0) 1865 314091
🖥 Visit the Heinemann Bookshop at www.heinemann.co.uk/library to browse our catalogue and order online.

First published in Great Britain by Heinemann Library, Halley Court, Jordan Hill, Oxford, OX2 8EJ, a division of Reed Educational and Professional Publishing Ltd.
Heinemann is a registered trademark of Reed Educational and Professional Publishing Ltd.

OXFORD MELBOURNE AUCKLAND
JOHANNESBURG BLANTYRE GABORONE
IBADAN PORTSMOUTH NH (USA) CHICAGO

Designed by Paul Davies and Associates
Originated by Ambassador Litho Ltd.
Printed at Wing King Tong in Hong Kong

ISBN 0 431 13070 1 (hardback)   ISBN 0 431 13077 9 (paperback)
06 05 04 03 02   06 05 04 03 02
10 9 8 7 6 5 4 3 2   10 9 8 7 6 5 4 3 2 1

British Library Cataloguing in Publication Data

Thomas, Roger, 1956-
  Brass. - (Soundbites)
  1.Brass instruments - Juvenile literature 2.Brass instrument music - Juvenile literature
  I.Title
  788.9

Northamptonshire Libraries & Information Service	
Peters	14-Oct-04
C788.9	£6.50

Acknowledgements

The Publishers would like to thank the following for permission to reproduce photographs: Corbis: Pg.10, Pg.15, Pg.19, Pg.26; Dat's Jazz Picture Library: Pg.27; Eyewire: Pg.5, Pg.7; Hutchinsons Picture Library: Pg.23; Jazz Index: Pg.25, Pg.29; Lebrecht Picture Library: Pg.12, Pg.17, Pg.18; Photodisc: Pg.7; Powerstock Zefa: Pg.22; Redferns: Pg.4, Pg.11, Pg.13, Pg.20, Pg.28; Trevor Clifford: Pg.8, Pg.9, Pg.14, Pg.16, Pg.21.

Cover photograph reproduced with permission of Trevor Clifford.

Every effort has been made to contact copyright holders of any material reproduced in this book. Any omissions will be rectified in subsequent printings if notice is given to the publishers.

The bugle has a long history of military use.

Brass, military and marching bands

Brass bands, **military** bands and marching bands can include all the instruments mentioned above, but there are also other more unusual brass instruments which are almost only used in this type of music. They include the cornet, which is also used in some pieces of classical music, the flugelhorn and the euphonium, which are both like the military bugle, and the mellophone.

Brass everywhere!

Brass instruments are used in many other kinds of music. The trumpet has been adopted by many musical cultures – for example, it is often used in Cuban music, and is usually the lead instrument in Mexican **mariachi** music. In classical music, there are groups called brass **ensembles** which feature a range of brass instruments. There are also wind bands and ensembles which include both brass and woodwind instruments.

In contemporary music, pieces are often written for an brass **soloist**, such as the'Sequenzas' written by the Italian Luciano Berio (1925–) or for several identical instruments, such as American Howard Johnson's jazz music for four or six tubas.

There are also instruments used in musical cultures around the world which work in the same way as brass instruments, but which are made of natural materials. For example, the aboriginal Australian didgeridoo is made from a tree-trunk which has been hollowed out by termites.

How do brass instruments work?

All brass instruments work in the same way. They consist of a long metal tube that has a cup-shaped **mouthpiece** at one end. The player presses his or her lips into the mouthpiece, keeping their lips tightly closed, then blows hard so that their lips vibrate. This makes the air in the tube vibrate, which makes a musical note. Getting this right is harder than it sounds!

Valves and slides

Because a tube of a certain length will only be able to make a few notes, lots of brass instruments, like trumpets, have valves that allow the air to move into extra pieces of tube. This means that the instruments can play a full range of notes. These valves are like taps in a water system and they work in the same way. There are two kinds: **piston valves** work by moving up and down, while **rotary valves** move from side to side.

The trombone is a bit different – it has a **slide**, a piece of tube that can be pulled out to make the instrument 'longer', thus changing the notes. The player changes the length of the trombone's tube by sliding a U-shaped length of tube in and out of the instrument while playing the instrument. This idea comes from the very earliest method of varying the notes of a brass instrument, when players had to have several extra pieces of tubing to 'plug into' the instrument.

What you hear is a bore...

The sound of a brass instrument is mainly projected outwards through the **bell**. An instrument's **tone** is mainly determined by how wide its tube (called the **bore**) is, and the shape of its bell. These factors are more important than the fact that the instruments are made out of metal. One musician once made a tuba out of cheese in order to prove this!

There are lots of different brass instruments, which can cover a very wide range of notes between them. This is one reason why groups consisting of nothing but brass instruments, such as brass bands, can play such a wide range of music.

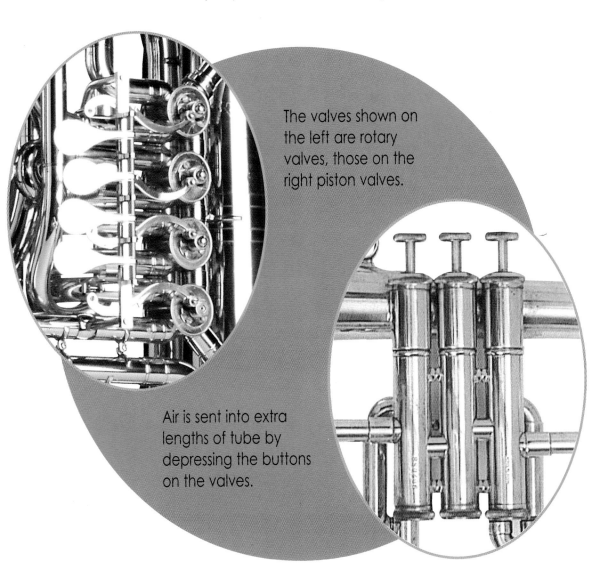

The valves shown on the left are rotary valves, those on the right piston valves.

Air is sent into extra lengths of tube by depressing the buttons on the valves.

Buzz lightly!

Lip pressure is very important when playing a brass instrument, so some players practise on a 'buzzer', which is really just a mouthpiece with a handle. If the player can 'buzz' a tune by getting the lip pressure for each note correct, then it will be easier to play it on a real instrument, with fewer noisy mistakes. It's also less stressful for anyone listening!

What do all the parts do?

Valved instruments

This picture shows a trumpet with the important parts named. The easiest way to look at the picture is to follow the path of the player's breath from the **mouthpiece** to the **bell**.

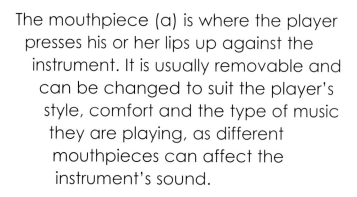

The mouthpiece (a) is where the player presses his or her lips up against the instrument. It is usually removable and can be changed to suit the player's style, comfort and the type of music they are playing, as different mouthpieces can affect the instrument's sound.

The mouthpipe (b) is the section of tube through which the player's breath passes before it reaches the valves.

The buttons (c) control which valves the player's breath passes through.

The water release valves (d) are not like the valves used to change the ranges of notes played on the instrument. They are really just covered holes, which can be opened in pauses during playing to let moisture out of the instrument – so be careful if you're standing in front of a trumpet player! These are also known as 'spit valves'.

The little finger hook (e) and the ring (f) are handles allowing the player to support the instrument.

The valves (g) allow air into extra pieces of tube to change the range of notes played on the instrument. You can see these extra pieces of tube attached to the valves.

The bell (h) is the flared open end of the main tube, where the sound of the instrument comes out.

All other brass instruments which have valves have similar parts which do the same jobs as the parts of a trumpet.

Slide instruments

Apart from the trombone family, the only other brass instrument in general use which has a **slide** to help the player change the notes is the slide trumpet, and even this is quite unusual. It looks much more like a small trombone than a normal trumpet.

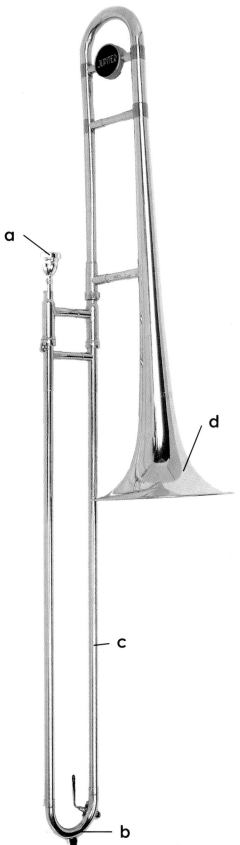

The picture on this page shows a trombone with the important parts named. This is the most usual kind, and is sometimes known as the **tenor** trombone. There is also an **alto** trombone, a **bass** trombone and a more unusual **contrabass** trombone. The bass and contrabass varieties also have a single **rotary valve** to let air into extra tubing to make the really low notes. There is also a valve trombone which has both a slide and three valves similar to those on a trumpet. The mouthpiece (a) is where the player presses his or her lips against the instrument. The water release valve (b) allows the player to release moisture from the instrument. The slide (c) is moved in and out, changing the length of the tube. The sound comes out through the bell (d).

9

The trumpet

The trumpet is perhaps the most widely-known of a group of similar instruments which also includes the cornet, the flugelhorn and the bugle. Instruments which worked in the same way as the trumpet were used more than two thousand years ago in ancient Egypt, Greece and Rome, as well as in other cultures across the world, and some of these designs still survive today. Unlike modern trumpets, which are made of brass, earlier trumpets were made of many different materials, such as animal horn, wood, tree bark or clay.

Medieval trumpets

One early form of the modern trumpet was the **buse**, a medieval instrument which was used for signalling. The long tube from which it was made was often made into a curved shape – this made it easier to carry and to play. This idea is still used in the design of most modern brass instruments.

How the modern trumpet developed

During the 17th and 18th centuries, the only way of getting a wide range of notes from a trumpet was by using two **mouthpieces** – one for high notes and one for low ones. Players tended to specialize in one or the other – the ones who played low notes were called 'principal blowers'. In the early 18th century, many instrument makers began thinking about ways of making it easier to play more notes on the instrument. One way was by having extra lengths of tubing

Horns like this were early versions of today's trumpet.

A typical modern trumpet.

(called 'crooks') which could be 'plugged into' the instrument, although this meant that the player had to stop playing while changing crooks! Another idea was to have one piece of tubing which slid in and out (a more modern form of this '**slide** trumpet' is still in use today). In about 1770, players started using the keyed trumpet, which had a tube with (usually) five holes in it.

However, although letting air out through the holes covered by the keys was like making the tube shorter, players still had to use several instruments with different tunings to get all the notes they needed. This eventually led to to the invention of the valve in around 1820, which allowed the air to pass into extra lengths of tube instead of just leaving the instrument 'early'. This design was the final major innovation which led to the trumpet we know today.

Fanfares

For special events, such as state occasions, special celebratory pieces called fanfares are sometimes written. These can be played on special trumpets called herald trumpets, like those shown in the picture (left), which have a very long **bell**. This helps the sound to project, and also looks quite impressive!

The trombone

The trombone was the first brass instrument to reach a form similar to that in use today. The main principle of the trombone is the use of a **slide**. This idea was first used in a **bass** trumpet some five hundred years ago.

Slides and valves

Although the slide trombone is the most widely used type of trombone – for example, it is always used in classical music – valve trombones also exist, which have instead a set of **piston valves** similar to those on a modern trumpet. The valve trombone is usually used by marching bands (for one thing, it is easier to operate a set of valves than a slide when you're marching!) and sometimes by jazz musicians.

Pitches and sizes

Originally, the trombone existed in a range of sizes, rather like the modern clarinet and saxophone families. Today, however, there are two types in common use – the **tenor** trombone (which is what people usually mean when they just refer to 'the trombone') and the bass trombone. The bass trombone plays lower notes. These are changed with a slide, although there is also a single valve at the back of the instrument which is used to reach a few notes.

However, some of the other sizes of trombone are still used occasionally. The **contrabass** trombone, which plays even lower notes than the bass trombone, is included in the music for some of Wagner's (1813–1883) operas. The smaller and higher-pitched **alto** trombone has been used by the German composer Beethoven (1770–1827) amongst many others.

a

This valve trombone has three piston valves (a).

12

The word 'trombone' shows how the instrument had its origins in the bass trumpet – it simply means 'big trumpet'. Jazz musicians would often play in street parades on open-topped trucks; trombonists would usually sit at the back of the vehicle to keep their slides out of the way, and so the trombone became known as the 'tailgate trombone'!

The trombone and jazz

Because it has a slide, the trombone is the only brass instrument which can produce a true **glissando**, which means gliding from one note to another instead of each note being sounded individually, like on a piano. This means that the trombone has a really expressive sound, which is one reason why it became popular as a jazz instrument early in music's history.

The trombone was a very popular instrument in early **big band** jazz.

The French horn

Is it really French?

Well, Count von Sporck of Bohemia, a nobleman who toured Europe in the early 1600s, seemed to think so when first heard it played in Paris. He had not seen such a horn before, and he thought that it was an instrument unique to France. Although there is no other proof that the instrument was invented in that country, the Count's conclusion could well be right, especially as the earliest use of the English term 'French horn' dates from the same period.

Playing the horn

The modern French horn is different from other valved instruments like the trumpet in several ways. It has **rotary valves**, which let air into different lengths of tube by being twisted sideways when the player presses the keys. It is also usually played with the player's fist inserted into the **bell**, which both muffles the sound slightly and changes the air pressure inside the instrument, which can help with playing some of the notes. This gives the instrument an unusual **tone**. It can sound gentle and even sad, but because of the length of tube, a good player can make it reach over four **octaves**.

The tube of the French horn is very long (up to 4.5 metres) and thin compared to other brass instruments. This makes it difficult to play, because it is harder to make such a long, thin column of air vibrate 'cleanly'.

The French horn's ancestors

The French horn – sometimes known as the orchestral horn, or just the horn – evolved from the signalling horns used widely by hunters and soldiers in Europe by the end of the 14th century. This connection survived for hundreds of years. For example, in around 1700, the German name *waldhorn* began to be used – it meant 'forest-horn'.

The earlier natural horn had no valves.

Various horn-like instruments were used during the Middle Ages and the **Renaissance**. Early horns (now known as natural horns) were of a fixed length, which meant that the player could not play a complete range of notes and had to use more than one horn, each of a different size. This problem was nearly solved by changing the design of the horn so that extra pieces of tubing could be 'plugged onto' the instrument. However, when valves were added to the horn in about 1850, it became possible for a single instrument to play a complete range without using extra tubing.

Old and new horns

Although the natural horn is still used in music specifically written for it (because of its pleasing soft tone), there are now various types of modern French horn in use in classical and orchestral music, in some areas of jazz and in marching bands. They include the double horn, which can be switched between two different tunings, and the smaller **descant horn**, which is an octave higher than the standard horn. There are also triple horns, which will cover all three tunings by using extra tubing.

The tuba

The tuba looks quite similar to other brass instruments – it consists of a long, conical metal tube with a **mouthpiece** and a set of valves. However, it is quite a modern instrument which only began to be developed in the early 19th century. It plays very low notes and is usually the lowest-**pitched** brass instrument in the orchestra.

The tuba plays very low notes.

When in Rome...

'Tuba' is a Latin word which was used by the Romans as a name for a type of military signalling trumpet which, confusingly, was nothing like the instrument we know today as the tuba. The development of the modern tuba was linked to the invention of the **piston valve** in around 1820, which made it possible to design instruments large enough to play very low notes, while at the same time making it possible to change the notes easily enough to play a **melody**.

Which came first?

One of the first tubas was developed in 1835 by Wilhelm Wieprecht, bandmaster of the Prussian Dragoon Guards, and an instrument maker from Berlin called Johann Gottfried Monitz. They had invented a brass instrument piston valve which was unusually wide, but still worked well. However, we do not know whether they invented the instrument first, then designed a valve to suit it, or whether they designed the valve first and then realized it would be ideal for a very big, low-pitched instrument.

A big family

The two inventors described their instrument as a '**bass** tuba', which seems to imply that they had the idea of making similar instruments of different sizes and pitches. Other makers certainly began to do this, so today there are many close relatives of the tuba, both larger and smaller. They include the euphonium and the sousaphone, which are discussed in the section on band instruments. However, there have been many variations on the tuba itself. One example is the **tenor** tuba, which became popular in France. Another very different example is the extraordinary sub-**contrabass** tuba ('contrabass' means 'below the bass', so 'sub-contrabass' means even lower than that), with a tube 10.5 metres long!

Wagner tuba

There are many other types. The Wagner tuba is one of the best known. The instrument is a mixture of several different instrument designs. In the late 1860s, the German composer Richard Wagner (1813–1883) was inspired by the instrument maker Adolphe Sax. Sax invented the saxophone, but also a brass instrument called the saxhorn. Wagner wanted a new kind of brass sound for his operas, so he commissioned a new instrument design which was something like the saxhorn and something like the tuba, but which had **rotary valves** like a French horn. This meant that it needed to be played in a similar way to the French horn, so the instruments are usually played by the orchestra's horn section.

The elegant-looking Wagner tuba was used in several of the composer's operas.

Band Instruments

Marching parade bands made up of wind and **percussion** instruments have existed in different forms for centuries. Originally they were attached to **military** regiments, but during the late 19th century, this type of music became more popular, and many different kinds of non-military bands were formed in the UK and America.

The European tradition

Brass bands are very popular in the UK and Europe, where they have traditionally got their players from a particular place. At the height of the industrial era, players came from a particular factory, company or **colliery**, where the band would also have a social function.

The American tradition

The tradition of marching and parade bands in America is also very strong, and rather different from the European tradition. The American tradition remains closer to its military origins, with many bands' uniforms being based on military dress, but the emphasis is very much on entertainment.

American bands can also include **majorettes**, who twirl batons in complicated patterns in time to the music. This idea has its origins in the role of the drum major, who marches at the front of a miltary band with a large baton.

A typical British brass band. Have you ever watched one play live?

Military bands

A full military band will include brass, woodwind and percussion. There are also smaller groups. These include those attached to cadet forces, which may be made up of just drums and bugles.

The instruments

It's not hard to see why the light glass-fibre sousaphone is a good idea!

These brass bands feature a much wider range of brass instruments than you can find either in orchestral or jazz music. Many innovations in designing musical instruments, such as the saxophone and the tuba, originated in military bands. This has resulted in a tradition which can include a variety of specialist instruments, many of which are hardly ever found elsewhere. Some marching band instruments are:

- The marching tuba, which has a **mouthpiece** positioned so that the tuba can be played while being carried comfortably on the shoulder instead of being held in front of the player. The **bell** may be made of **glass-fibre**, which is lighter than brass.
- The sousaphone, which is a form of **bass** tuba which was suggested by and named after the famous 19th century American composer and bandmaster John Philip Sousa. It has a special circular shape which allows the player to 'wear' it by resting it on one shoulder. Many are made with a glass-fibre main tube and bell (like the marching tuba) to make them lighter.

More band instruments

More instruments

There are even more band instruments in the middle and upper **registers**. Some of these instruments are also sometimes used in orchestral music and jazz.

- The EUPHONIUM – This is also used in orchestral music, where it is usually called a **tenor** tuba. It is quite like a tuba in shape, but smaller, although it is said to be derived from the **bass** saxhorn (see the saxhorn entry). It is a particularly important instrument in British brass bands, where it is often used as a **solo** instrument. It has a smooth, rich **tone**. The instrument's name comes from a Greek word which means 'having a pleasing sound'.

- The FLUGELHORN – This instrument looks a little bit like a trumpet, but was in fact developed from the keyed bugle (a military bugle with keys added to help change the notes) in Vienna in the 1820s. The flugelhorn worked better because of its valves and extra lengths of tube, and proved to be much more popular.

Marching bands in America use lots of different specialized instruments.

- The MELLOPHONE – This instrument also has a similar shape to a trumpet, but was in fact derived from the French horn. This influence can be seen in the design of the **bell** of the mellophone, which is very wide.

- The CORNET – This instrument, which dates from around 1820, is very important in brass and marching bands. It is related to the flugelhorn, but its sound is between that of a trumpet and a French horn.

- The BUGLE – The bugle is based on the traditional military signalling instrument. A basic bugle is like a small natural trumpet (it has no keys or valves).

- The SAXHORN – This family of brass instruments was invented by the Belgian Adolphe Sax in 1845. Sax created nine different sizes of saxhorn, covering the whole **pitch**

The tenor horn is just one of the specialized marching band instruments.

range from **sopranino** (for very high notes) to 'sub-bass', which means even lower than the usual bass range. Some were designed to be held horizontally, like the trumpet, while others were held vertically, like the tuba, depending on size.

Still more instruments!

There are and have been many more types of band instrument, particularly in America. They include the **clavicor**, the valve trombone (there is also an 'upright' version of this which is easier to march with), the bass trumpet, the **cornopean** and **alto** French horn (both slightly similar in appearance to the flugelhorn) and many others.

Historical and non-Western brass and horns

'Brass' which isn't brass

Even today, many brass instruments are not made of proper brass. There can be many reasons for using different materials. Sometimes this is done to make the instruments lighter, like the **glass-fibre** marching band instruments (see pages 18–19), or to make the instruments cheaper – some beginners' trumpets, for example, have plastic valve casings.

The shofar was probably the instrument described in the Bible story of Joshua, who used musical sound to shake down the walls of Jericho.

However, before people learned how to extract metals from **metal ores**, many other materials were used to make instruments which worked in a similar way to modern brass instruments. Many of these instruments evolved in non-**Western** cultures, and many are still used today. These 'pre-brass' instruments include:

- The DIDGERIDOO – This is a traditional aboriginal Australian instrument. Authentic didgeridoos are made from long tree trunks which have been hollowed out by termites. A circular **mouthpiece** made from beeswax is attached to one end. The player presses his or her lips to the mouthpiece and produces the instrument's unusual sound by blowing into the instrument so that their lips vibrate. The player can produce a few different notes by varying the amount of lip pressure and the amount of air blown into the instrument.

- The SHOFAR – Hollowed-out animal horns have been used as trumpet-like instruments across many cultures throughout history. This traditional instrument is mainly used in Jewish religious ceremonies. It is made from the horn of a ram.

The South American continent has a rich tradition of trumpet-like instruments made from different materials, including clay (Peru), gold (Colombia) and even human bone!

The Tibetan trumpet has a unique sound!

Brass, bronze and other metal instruments

- TIBETAN TRUMPET – This large metal trumpet used in religious ceremonies has a unique sound.
- The LUR – This is an unusual historical instrument, examples of which have survived in Scandinavia since the Bronze Age (and these examples were actually made of bronze). It is a large, curved instrument with a **bell** which is covered by a flat disc. The sound comes out through a single small hole in the centre of the disc. The mouthpiece is similar to that of the modern trombone.
- CHINESE FUNERAL TRUMPETS – These very long trumpets are used in traditional funeral processions. There are both straight and curved types. They are cleverly designed to be collapsed like a telescope when they are not being used.

What's in a name?

The tromba marina was an 18th century instrument – its name means 'marine trumpet'. It was actually a string instrument, and had nothing to do with the sea. Also, if you play the tuba and decide you might like to try playing the tubaphone, remember that the tubaphone is in fact a **percussion** instrument!

Brass and jazz

Although other instruments like the saxophone are very prominent in jazz today, the trumpet, cornet and trombone were the most important '**front line**' instruments during the early history of the music. One of the explanations suggested for this is the wide availability in America of second-hand brass instruments at the end of the 19th century. This was because when the American Civil War ended, there were far fewer musicians playing in **military** bands. The immediate result of this was that town bands were formed, which were similar in some ways to marching military bands. This tradition survives today in the American city of New Orleans.

From street to stage

These musicians then began to be hired to play in smaller bands which were a better size for the **cabarets** and gambling clubs of New Orleans. The city was a busy seaport and had many establishments like these to provide entertainment for off-duty sailors. By the 1920s, the style which we would now call jazz had become recognizable, and jazz brass players began to attract a following.

History and progress

By examining surviving documents, photographs and recordings from this period, we can learn a great deal about how brass instruments were used in early jazz. For example, there is a photograph of the band led by the famous cornetist Buddy Bolden (1877–1931) which shows his trombonist carrying a valve trombone (see pages 9–12) instead of the **slide** trombone which is more widely used today. This was a direct result of jazz's connections with military bands, as the valve trombone was usually used in American military bands at that time.

The trumpet and cornet were the instruments of the **virtuoso** during this period, as their high **pitch** and bright **tone** made them suitable for playing solos which could 'carry' above the rest of the band. The trombone tended to have a supporting role. Other brass instruments which had originated in military

bands also found their way into jazz, such as the tuba or sousaphone (see pages 16–19), which would play the **bass part**. This role has survived in modern music in an interesting way, as some expert **contemporary bass** players, such as Herbie Flowers, play double bass, bass guitar and tuba.

This photograph shows several brass instruments being used in early jazz.

Modern jazz brass

As the decades passed, many virtuoso jazz brass players added their own influences to the music, such as the trumpet and cornet player Louis Armstrong (1900–1971) and the trumpet players Miles Davis (1926–1991) and Dizzy Gillespie (1917–1993). Brass instruments are now used in all forms of jazz. These include traditional bands, **big bands** (which will normally have sections of trumpets and trombones) and contemporary small bands which will often be more flexible in their line-ups. For example, such a band may be led by a trombonist, or feature two identical brass instruments, or include instruments such as the **tenor** horn which are more usually associated with brass bands and marching bands.

25

Brass instruments and recording/performance technology

Brass instruments have several important roles within **contemporary** rock and pop music, and this is reflected in the way in which they are used on stage and in the production of recordings. Also, the nature of jazz, rock and pop performances has changed enormously, with audiences expecting much more. All of these problems are dealt with by modern electronic and **acoustic** technology, and it is important for modern brass players who work in these areas to have at least a little bit of understanding of these subjects.

Brass onstage

There are lots of situations in which brass instruments will need to be **amplified** for use onstage. This may apply to a jazz **soloist** playing to a large audience, to a horn section backing a rock band, or to a light orchestra or **big band**. In each case, there are two main ways of amplifying brass instruments: one or more microphones can be set up in front of the player, or a microphone can be attached to the instrument itself. The signals from the microphone are then fed to a **mixer**, which is used to balance the sound with the other instruments and voices onstage. The mixture of signals then passes to an amplifier and loudspeakers, which make the overall sound as loud as necessary.

One way of making brass instruments louder is a separate microphone.

Brass and microphones

There are advantages and disadvantages to both kinds of microphone. A microphone standing in front of the player lets the player control the instrument's sound more easily. For example, a trombonist playing a very long note can gradually move the **bell** of the instrument towards the microphone as he or she starts to run out of breath. This means that, while the player may be unable to play as loudly at the end of the note as at the beginning, the audience will not notice because the microphone will gradually make up for this as the trombonist moves towards it. Also, sometimes two or more brass players can share a single microphone, which allows the sounds of their instruments to blend naturally before they reach the mixer.

Another way is to fix the microphone to the instrument.

A microphone attached directly to the instrument is more suitable for soloists. For example, it allows the sound of the instrument to be easily processed through electronic effects such as **echo**, which the player can control onstage with **foot pedals**. However, because the position of the instrument to the microphone cannot be changed during a performance, all changes in the instrument's sound – even simple ones, such as volume – have to be controlled electronically, either by the performer or by the **sound engineer**.

Brass in the studio

Microphones and amplification are also used when studio recordings featuring brass instruments are made. Often, however, the engineer will aim to get a consistent sound from the soloist or section, because any variations in volume, plus sound effects such as reverberation ('reverb', which adds a slight, live-sounding echo to the signal) can be added later.

Brass transformed

Brass instruments are simple in construction in comparison with, for example, a **pipe organ**. In a sense, brass instruments do not create any sound at all – they really change and **amplify** the sound made by the player's lips.

However, many brass players have invented their own ways of making these instruments produce completely new sounds. Traditionally this has been achieved by using different types of playing techniques and **mutes**. Most of these new ideas have occurred in jazz and **avant-garde** music. Many of them involve the use of electronics to change the sound of the instrument, while others use simple materials and everyday objects to change the instrument's tone.

Miles Davis and his 'plugged-in' trumpet. The microphone is attached to the front of the instrument.

Miles Davis

In the late 1960s, the African-American jazz trumpet player Miles Davis (1926–1991) adopted a new approach to the instrument. He not only played it with a mute for most of the time, but he also attached a microphone to it. This was not just to make the instrument louder – it also allowed him to send the sound of the trumpet through electronic effects such as a 'wah-wah' pedal usually used by electric guitar players. This gave the instrument an entirely new range of sounds. Many listeners who preferred more traditional jazz were not pleased!

Another trombonist, Radu Malfatti, changes the sound of his instrument by using unusual mutes, such as a small Chinese drum or a tennis ball (shown here).

Other innovations

Since the time of Miles Davis, musicians and instrument makers have continued to experiment with ways of extending the sounds of brass instruments. Here are a few examples:

• Yamaha produced the Electronic Valve Instrument – EVI for short – which makes no sound itself, but which can be electronically connected to **MIDI** sound modules. The player's breath and the 'valves' control the sound depending on how the electronics are set up.

• The trombonist Nic Collins modified his instrument in a similar way.

• The tuba player Melvyn Poore sometimes plays his instrument through a saxophone mouthpiece.

• The trumpet player John Corbett wraps the **bell** of his instrument in kitchen foil to create a buzzing tone.

• The avant-garde composer and musician Vinko Globokar sometimes treats his trombone as a **percussion** instrument by scraping the bell along the floor. Don't try this with your instrument without permission!

Several other musical instrument companies have marketed other interesting and unusual ideas for brass players. These have included trumpets with interchangeable bells and small inserts which fit into the mouthpiece. Both change the instrument's **tone**. With so many different approaches to this group of instruments, there will always be room for new ideas.

Glossary

acoustic relating to sound, or, when used of instruments, unamplified

alto a pitch range lower than soprano but higher than tenor

amplify/ied made louder, usually electronically

avant-garde modern and experimental

bass refers to the lowest range of notes in normal use (contrabass and subcontrabass are lower still) – when used to describe an instrument or voice, the term means lower than

baritone a low pitch range, above bass

bass part the part of a composition written for a bass instrument

bell the flared end of a brass instrument through which the sound emerges

big band a large jazz orchestra

bore the hollow area within the tube of a wind instrument

buse an early brass instrument

cabaret musical entertainment held in a night-club or restaurant

clavicor a brass band instrument from the 19th century

colliery a coal mine

contemporary of the present day

contrabass lower than bass

cornopean a brass band instrument from the 19th century

descant horn a high-pitched type of French horn

echo a repeat of a sound caused by the noise reflecting back to the listener

ensemble a musical group which is smaller than an orchestra

foot pedals foot-controlled electronic devices which change amplified sound

front line the main melody instruments in a jazz or rock band

glass-fibre a substance made from strands of glass which, when mixed with a resin, form a hard but lightweight material

glissando 'sliding' form one note to another

majorettes female parade marchers who carry batons with which they perform intricate movements

mariachi a form of traditional Mexican music

melody the main tune in a piece of music

metal ores rocks from which metals are extracted by crushing and heating

MIDI stands for Musical Instrument Digital Interface; a type of computer language which allows some electronic instruments to exchange data with computers and with each other

military to do with the armed forces

mixer an electronic device which blends the sounds from microphones or electronic instruments

mouthpiece part of the instrument through which the player blows

mute a device inserted into the bell of a brass instrument which changes its sound

octave a sequence of eight whole notes

percussion instruments played by striking (or, in a few cases, friction)

pipe organ a keyboard instrument which produces sound by forcing air through large, flute-like pipes

piston valves valves which operate with an up-and-down movement

pitch how high or low a note is

reed a small piece of cane which vibrates when air is blown across it

register the group of notes which an instrument can reach when it is played

Renaissance the artistic and cultural revival in Europe during the 14th, 15th and 16th centuries

rotary valves valves which operate by turning from side to side

slide a section of tube on a brass instrument which is moved in and out to change the notes

solo/ist a section or piece of music featuring a single instrument or played by a single musician alone; a musician playing such music

sopranino higher in pitch than soprano

soprano a pitch range higher than alto but lower than sopranino – the highest range in general use

sound engineer a technician who deals with the recording or amplification of music

tenor a pitch range which is lower than alto but higher than baritone

tone the quality of a sound, often described in visual terms – bright, dark etc.

virtuoso a musician of exceptional ability

wah-wah a type of tone produced by moving a mute in and out of a brass instrument or electronically by using a foot pedal

woodwind the group of instruments which includes flutes, clarinets and saxophones

Index